A Wounded Gal's Feelings

Zionna Renea

Presentation by *BookLeaf Publishing*

Web: www.bookleafpub.com

E-mail: info@bookleafpub.com

ISBN: 9789357691093

First edition 2022

Dear Younger Self

the hurt and pain you may feel now, will soon
diminish
but always remember,
you must first get uncomfortable to change.

No longer your little girl.

lately i've been trying to figure out the right
words to say to you,

how to explain that I'm not who you think I am,

I can't be who you want me to be

I know what I want, and who I am becoming

it is and always will be my decision.

Abuse

Its the audacity of our elders
to dictate how we act
what we say
what we wear

many of us lose our voice at such a young age

we shield our emotions, words, and feelings

because we are told to

"mind your mouth"

"stay in a child's place"

"Don't speak unless you're spoken to"

Facade

In order for Her to feel safe
to save herself from feeling vulnerable
She became a different part for Her

She had become someone that
was hard to get rid of
Let alone someone Her appreciated.

She rebuilt the walls that would fall
and Her would refused to cry

There was a love-hate relationship between the
two,
but without this facade,

Would Her have survived ?

Where I'm from

5

the almighty God is the most powerful
    and
the color of my skin is an issue
— to some

the south is full of warm winters,
the local night traditions, ah
the skating, slushies
waffles and wings

The children are invisible
the invisible are talented

the books clouded my reality
the music clouded their mentality
the unshed-den tears build up

your biggest dream is to escape
your fantasy becomes reachable
your potential becomes unleashed

Me

nobody has ever let me be me,
for me to even know who I am.

they babied me forever, and still continue to.

I grew up way before they'd known
there was pain a 10 yr old couldn't deal with
alone

sleepless nights of soft sorrows

my pain was a problem
something I was punished and yelled at for

I remember everything

I still blame all of you

I'm crying more frequently, because the pain is
still there
I don't know how to say anything
I get shut out for everything
I feel broken even more than before
the small things push me over because, the big
things

are so far from interpretation

nobody knows me
I don't know me

13 years

you were always there for me
the only one that really understood me.

in year four, I moved away causing for us to drift
slightly
then it became a thing where I would move
further, but we became stronger.

highschool began and nothing could stop us
every weekend we would be together.

your family became mine
at times they treated me better than my own.

no matter the circumstances you were my
everything.

year eleven came and things began to change
by year twelve we had our share of arguments
but then came the boy and girl that would hurt
us forever

I later learned, yes they were at fault,
but so were you and I

I loved you unconditionally,
but allowed you to treat me despicably,

and I hope all the loved you shared was not a
game,

but even if so, I regret no small or big thing .

I will forever have a place for you in my heart,
because you really were a big part of my life.

Insanity

having a full day of great things means nothing,
when ending your day in a toxic environment.

it will always have an affect on you.

how are you expected to grow,
when your foundation and safe place are tainted.

Life Path

trust that you know what is meant to be,
and expected of you, through your eyes.

trust your thoughts, decisions, and intuition.

trust in yourself to know your path

to know what's meant of you,

because only you can truly decide.

Change

even in your toughest times,
you're not where you use to be,
life is better in some aspect of your life,
big or small.

you are further than you were before.

Feelings

CRY!

Cry about it.
feel every single emotion,
and let it all out.

Say no

To the ones who were not allowed to #sayno

I'm sorry,
sorry that no one was there for you
sorry that you had to deal with the pain alone
sorry that they blamed you
sorry that you blamed you

you deserve more.

Tired

I'm tired

tired of doing what is not appreciated

tired of not being happy

tired of waking up wishing for a new

tired of doing more for others than myself.

Thankfully I'm Readily Exchanging the Dread

for a middle finger in the air.

Guidance

Life is unexpectedly changing every day,
the stress of it all can cause a turmoil of distrust.

The ability to trust is exceptional.
To trust in yourself
is the ability to create,

to turn your dreams into reality.

Remember

sometimes you just have to sit back,
take a deep breath,
and remind yourself
that you are capable of anything you set your
mind to.

Its not me, Its you

Despite the love I have for you all,
and the love you think you may show,

I think you should know,

that I'm not sure if I respect you.

Many have put me down

or ignored my cries,

and while my everyday goal is to hide behind

the smile, you all seem to love so much,

inside I'm slowly falling apart.

Love Grows

The journey of loving you has been chaotic,

But I wouldn't change it for the world.

I love you wholeheartedly, and I

Promise to tell you every chance I get.

Especially every morning when I look into the mirror.

Happy Ever After

You are capable of overcoming
any hardships.

whether it be
mentally,
emotionally,
physically, or socially.

You deserve to live your fairytale.
every day that you show up for yourself,
you are a step closer to achieving your dreams.